Dedicated to my cherished family - Nile, Kai, and Jason, may this story enrich your understanding and appreciation of a beautiful tradition. This book is a bilingual journey, lovingly created with the assistance from Midjourney and ChatGPT.

With love,
Ying

献给我亲爱的家人 - Nile, Kai和Jason，愿这个故事增进你们对美丽传统的理解和欣赏。这是一本在Midjourney和ChatGPT的协助下用爱创作的双语书籍。

爱你们的，
王迎

© 2024 Ying Wang. All rights reserved. No part of this publication may be reproduced or transmitted in any form or by any means, electronic or mechanical, including photocopying, recording, or any information storage and retrieval system, without permission in writing from the writer or publisher.

The Tale of Nian
A Lunar New Year Story
年的故事 一个春节的传说

By Ying Wang 王迎 / 著

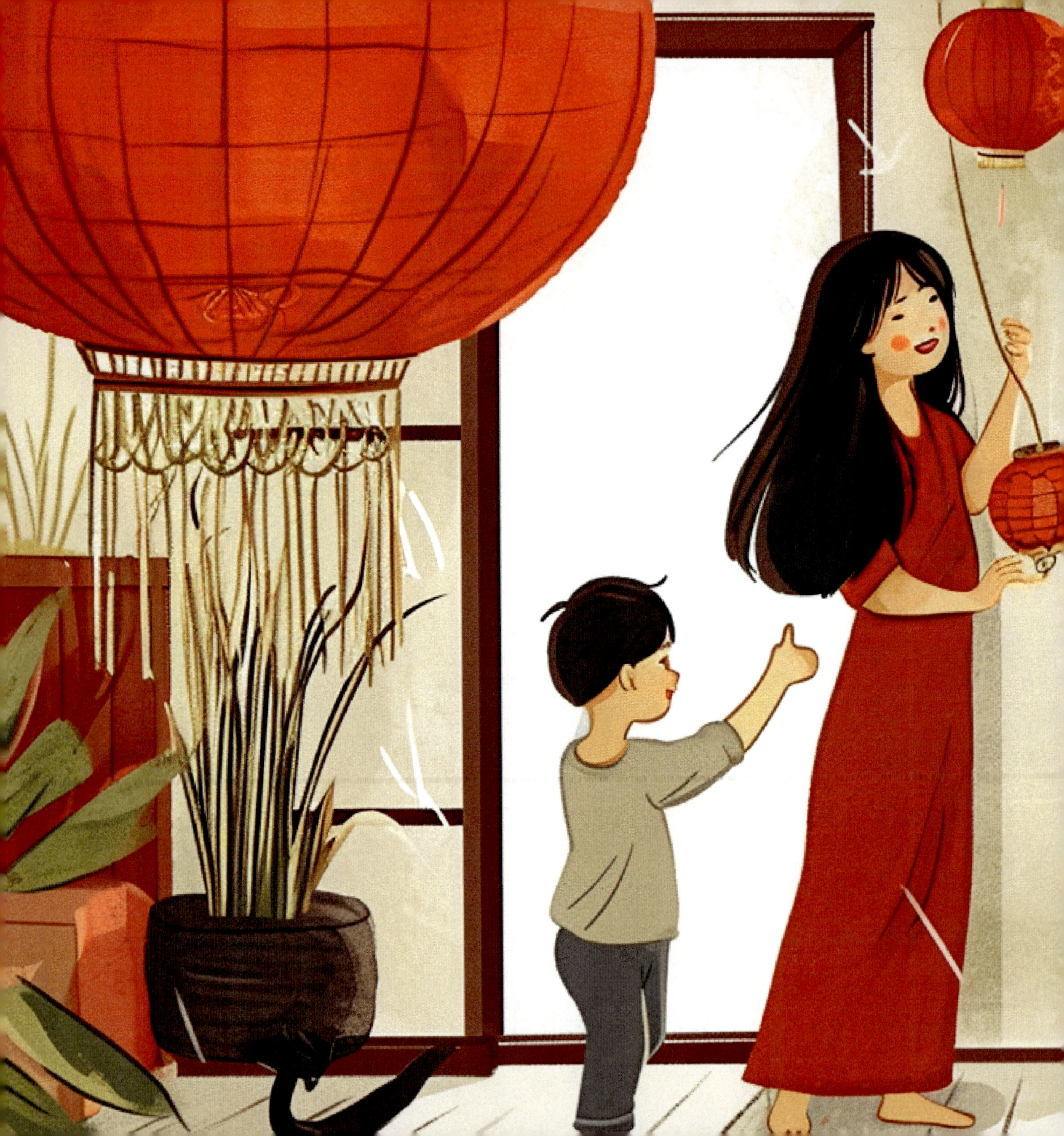

Lunar New Year is almost here! Nico and Keen are helping their mom to decorate their living room. Nico asks mom "Why are all the decorations red?"

春节快到了！尼克和凯恩在帮妈妈装饰客厅。尼克问妈妈："为什么所有的装饰品都是红色的？"

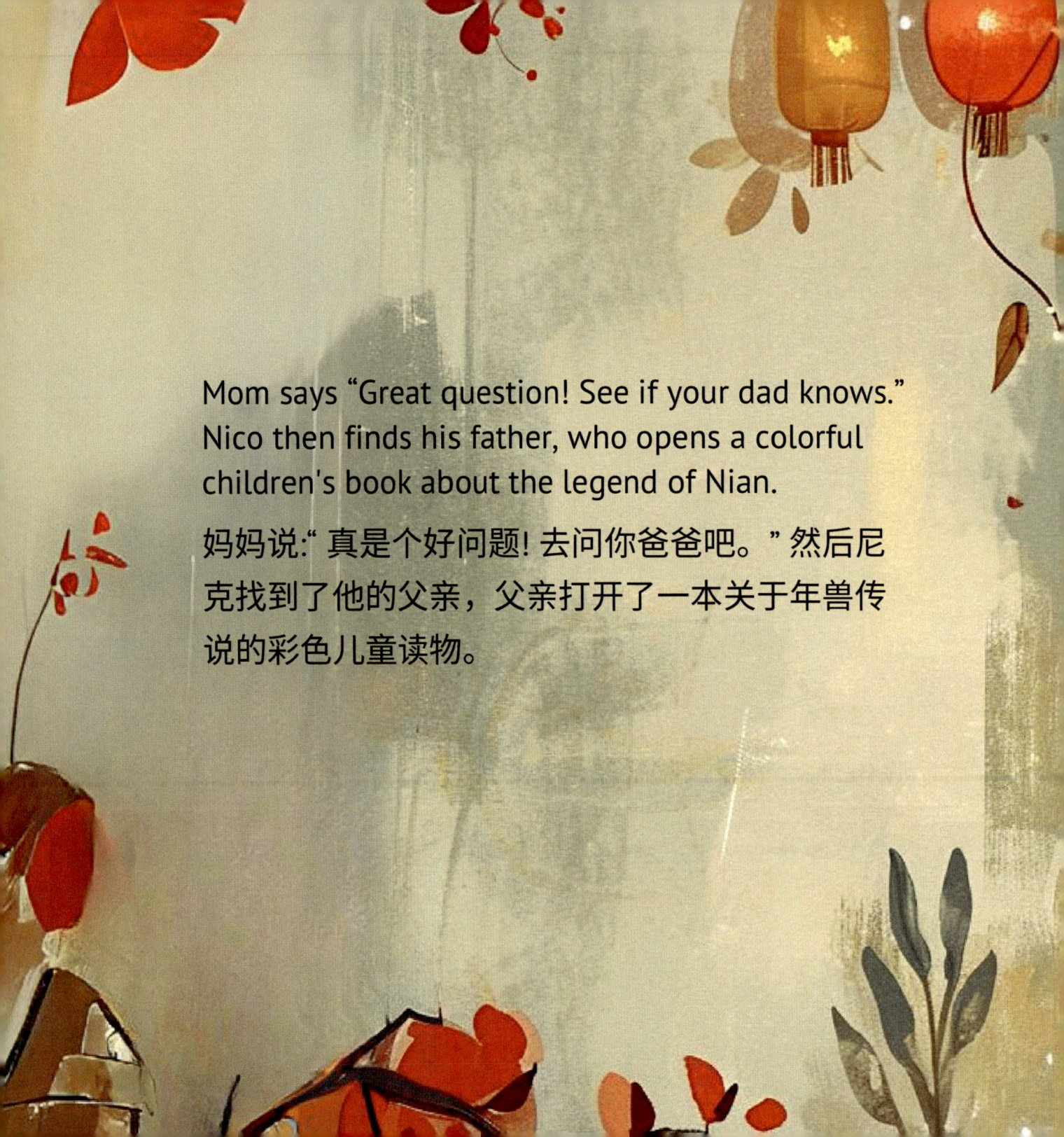

Mom says "Great question! See if your dad knows." Nico then finds his father, who opens a colorful children's book about the legend of Nian.

妈妈说:" 真是个好问题! 去问你爸爸吧。" 然后尼克找到了他的父亲，父亲打开了一本关于年兽传说的彩色儿童读物。

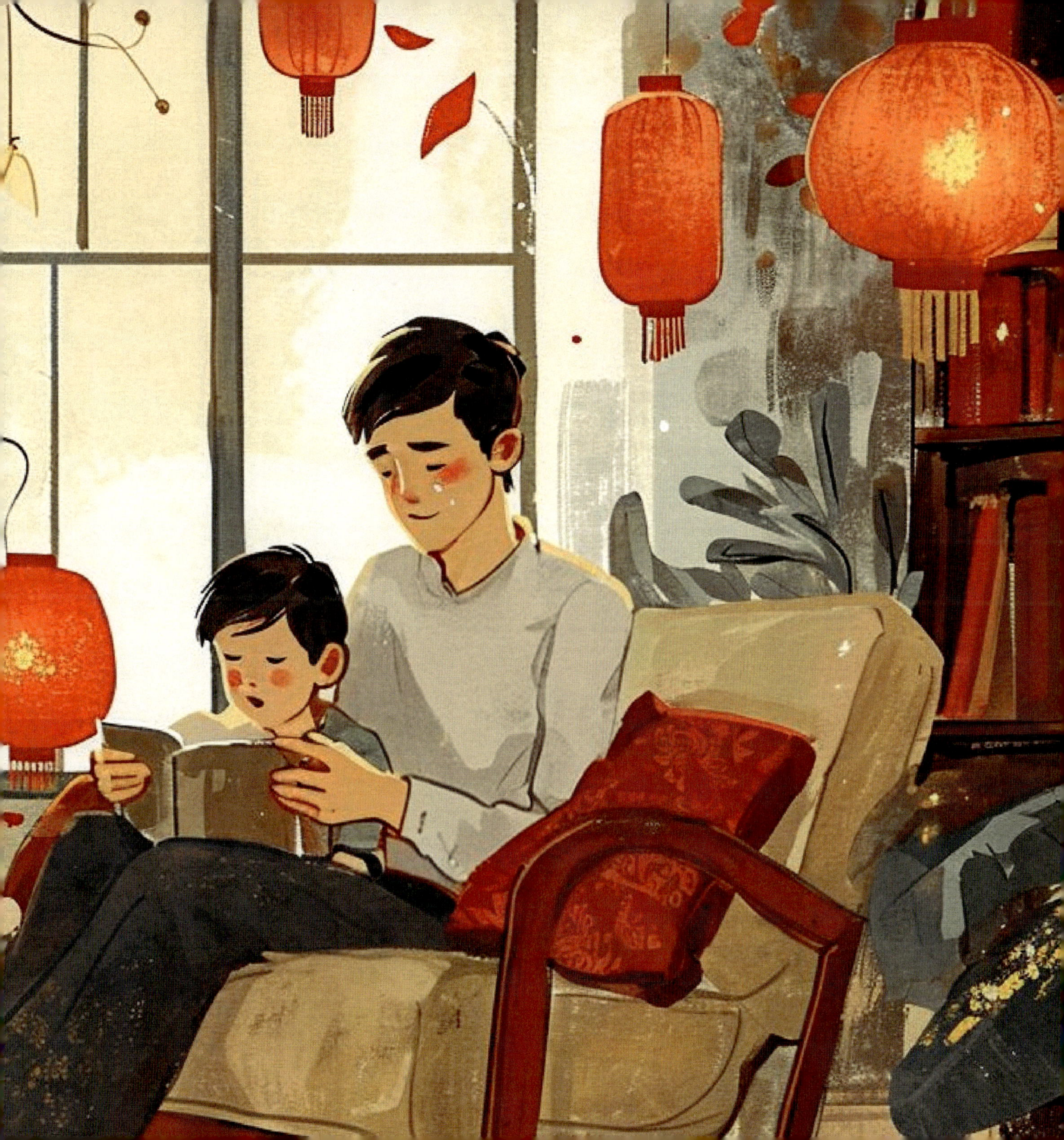

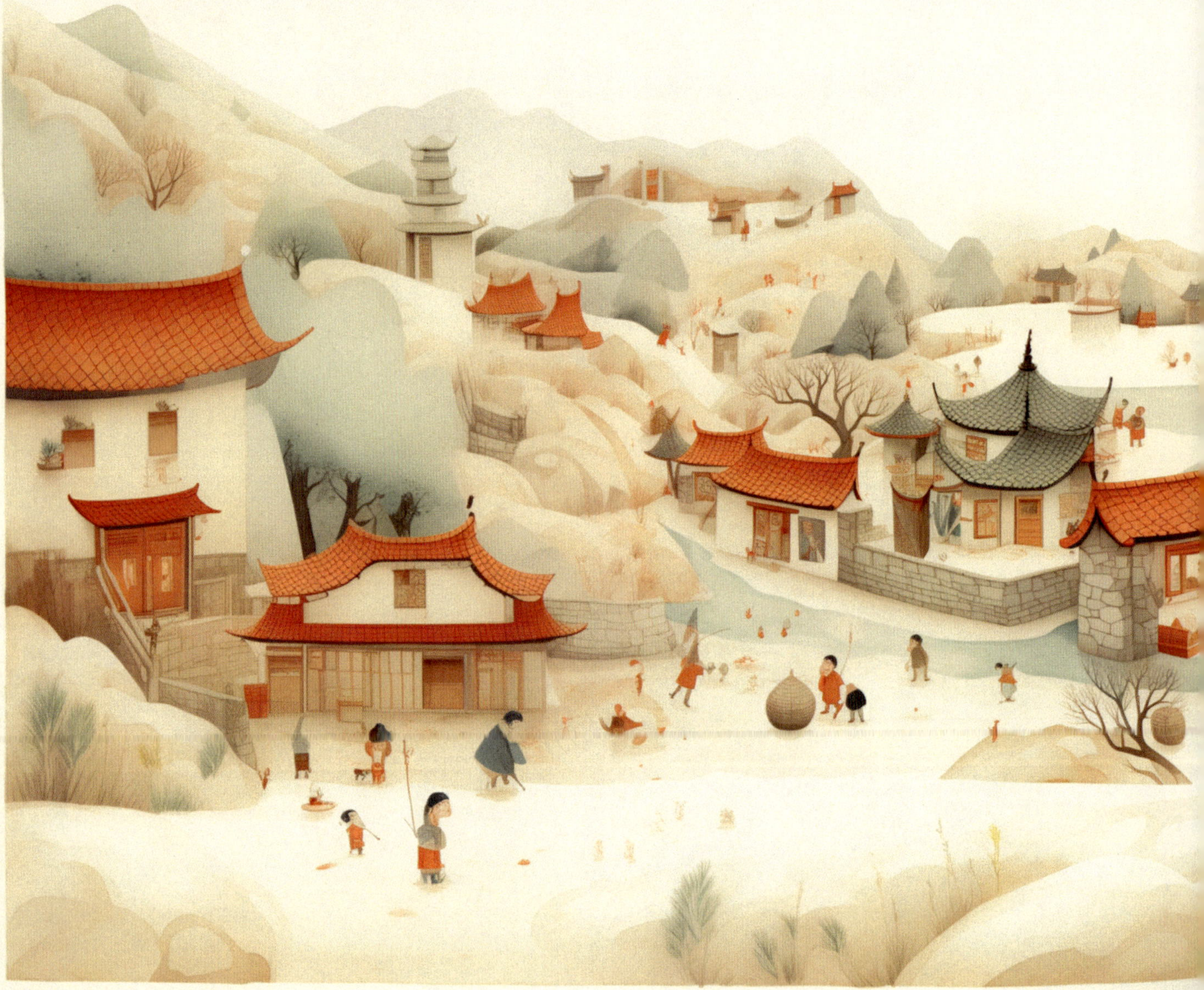

Once upon a time there was a peaceful Chinese village.
很久很久以前有一个和平的村落。

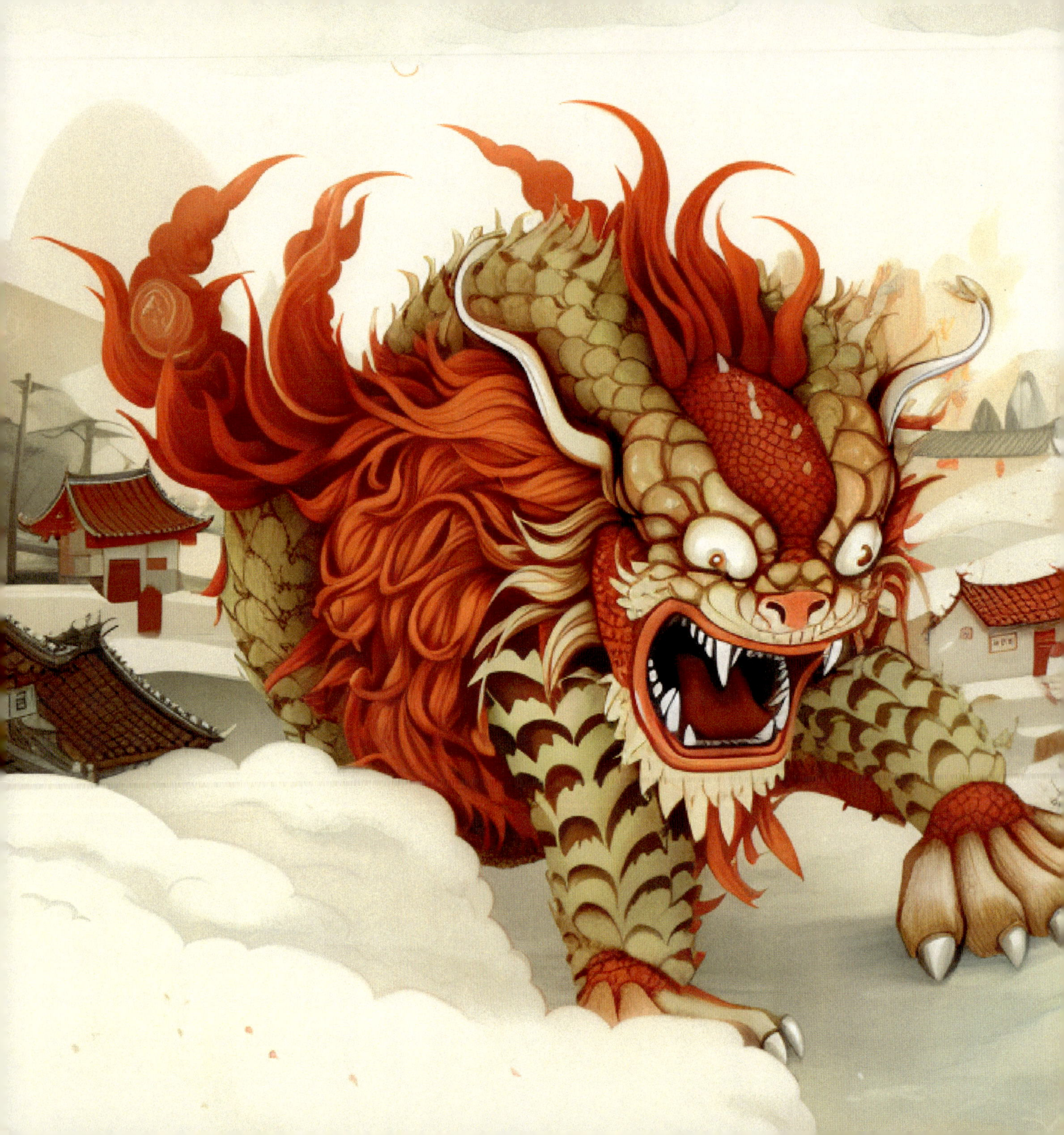

Every year right before the Lunar New Year, a big, scary beast called Nian would appear near the village. Nian looked like a mix of a dragon and a lion, making the villagers hide indoors.

每到农历新年前夕，一只又大又可怕的野兽'年'就会出现。它长得既像龙又像狮子，吓得村民们都躲进了家里。

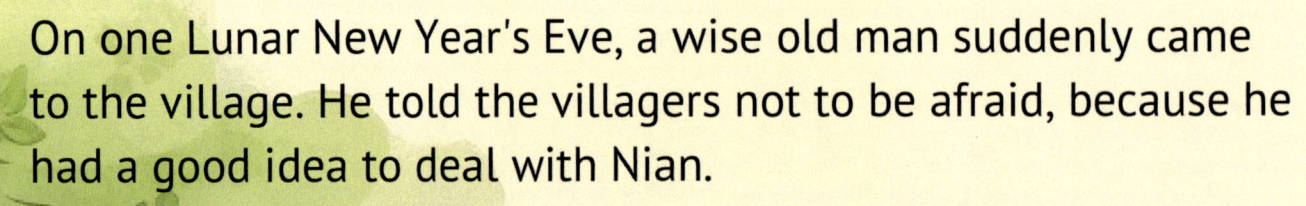

On one Lunar New Year's Eve, a wise old man suddenly came to the village. He told the villagers not to be afraid, because he had a good idea to deal with Nian.

有一年除夕之夜，村子里突然来了一位智慧的老人。他告诉村民们不要怕，因为他有对付年的好主意。

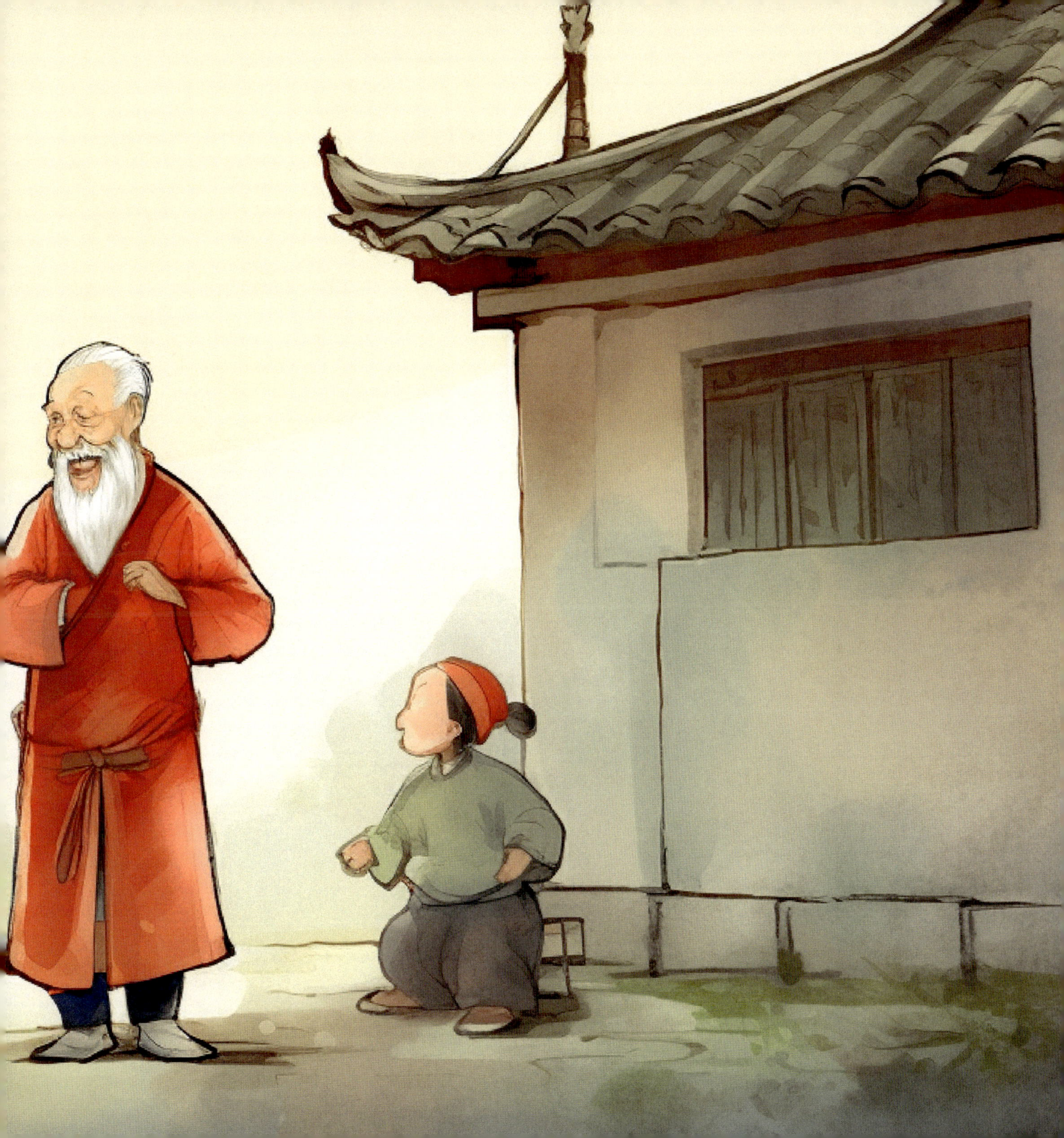

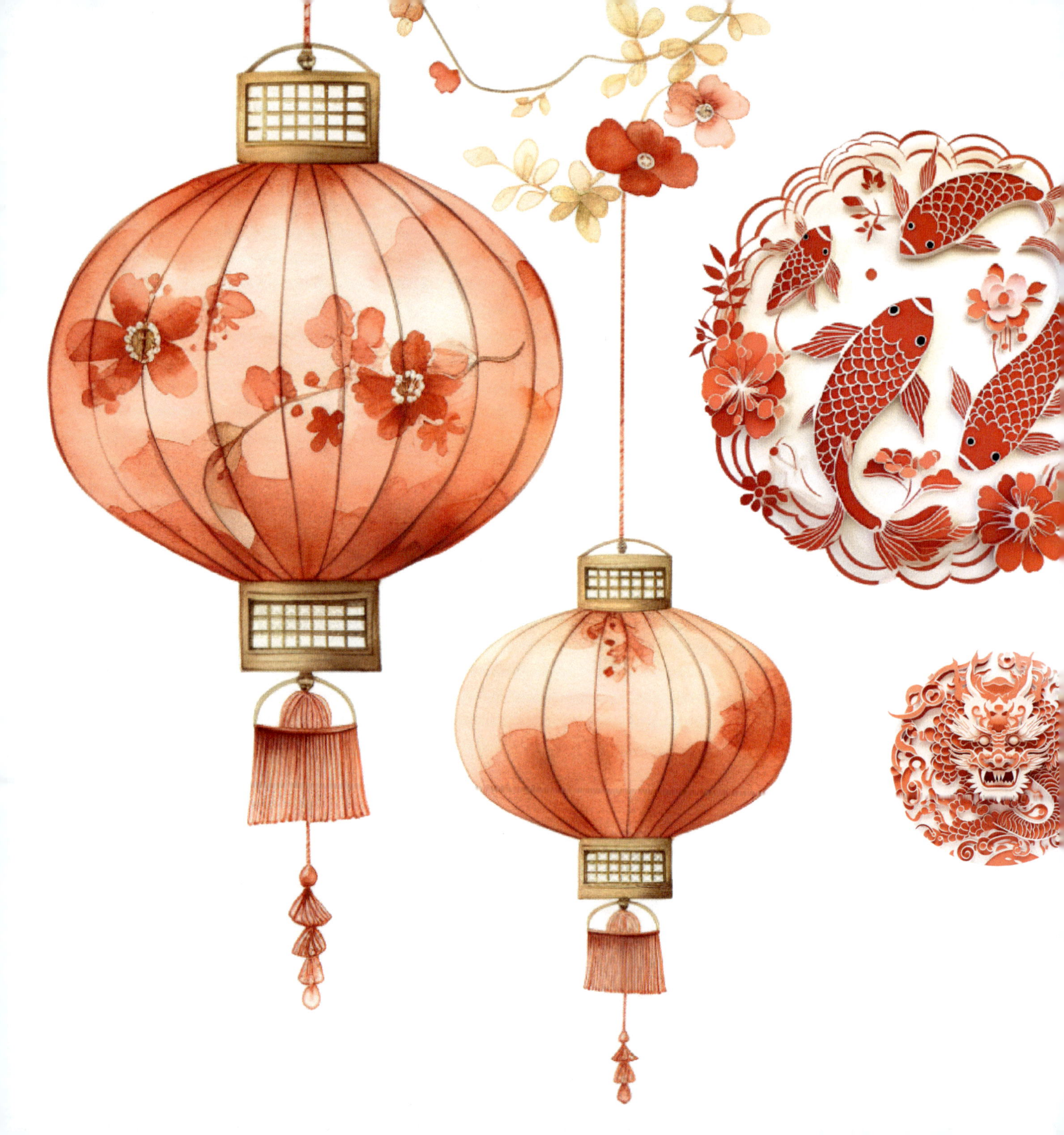

The old man quietly took out red lanterns, paper-cut for window decoration, and firecrackers and told the villagers to use these red decorations to drive away Nian.

这个老人不慌不忙地从衣服里拿出了红灯笼，窗花和鞭炮并告诉村民们用这些红色装饰来赶走'年'。

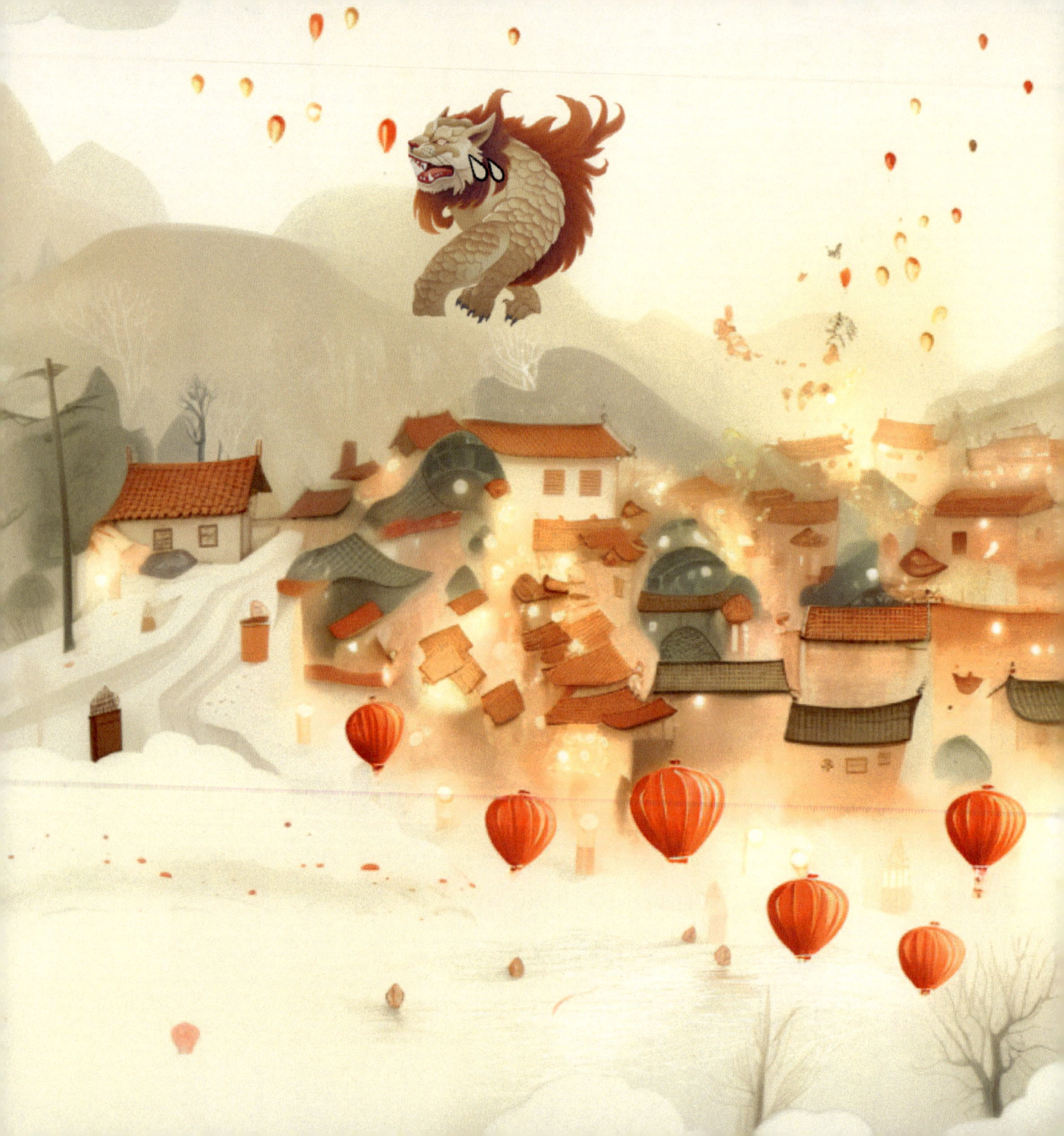

Sure enough, Nian, scared by the red decorations and loud noises, fled into the night.

果然'年'被红色装饰和响声吓到，一溜烟地逃走了。

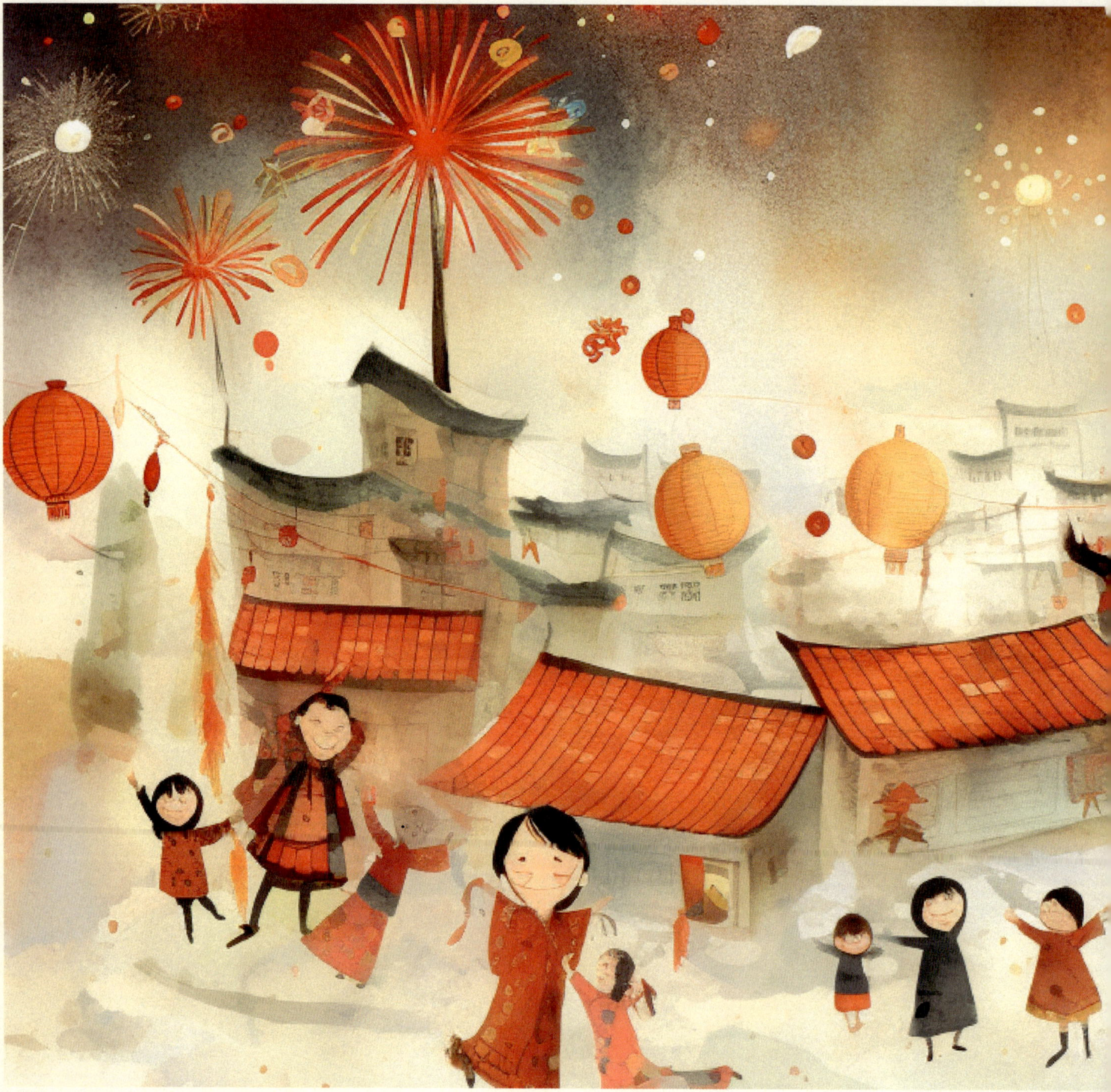

The villagers celebrated the victory over Nian. Since then, every Lunar New Year has been marked with red decorations and loud fireworks.

村民们庆祝了打败'年'的胜利。从那以后，每逢春节，家家户户都会挂上红色装饰，放响鞭炮。

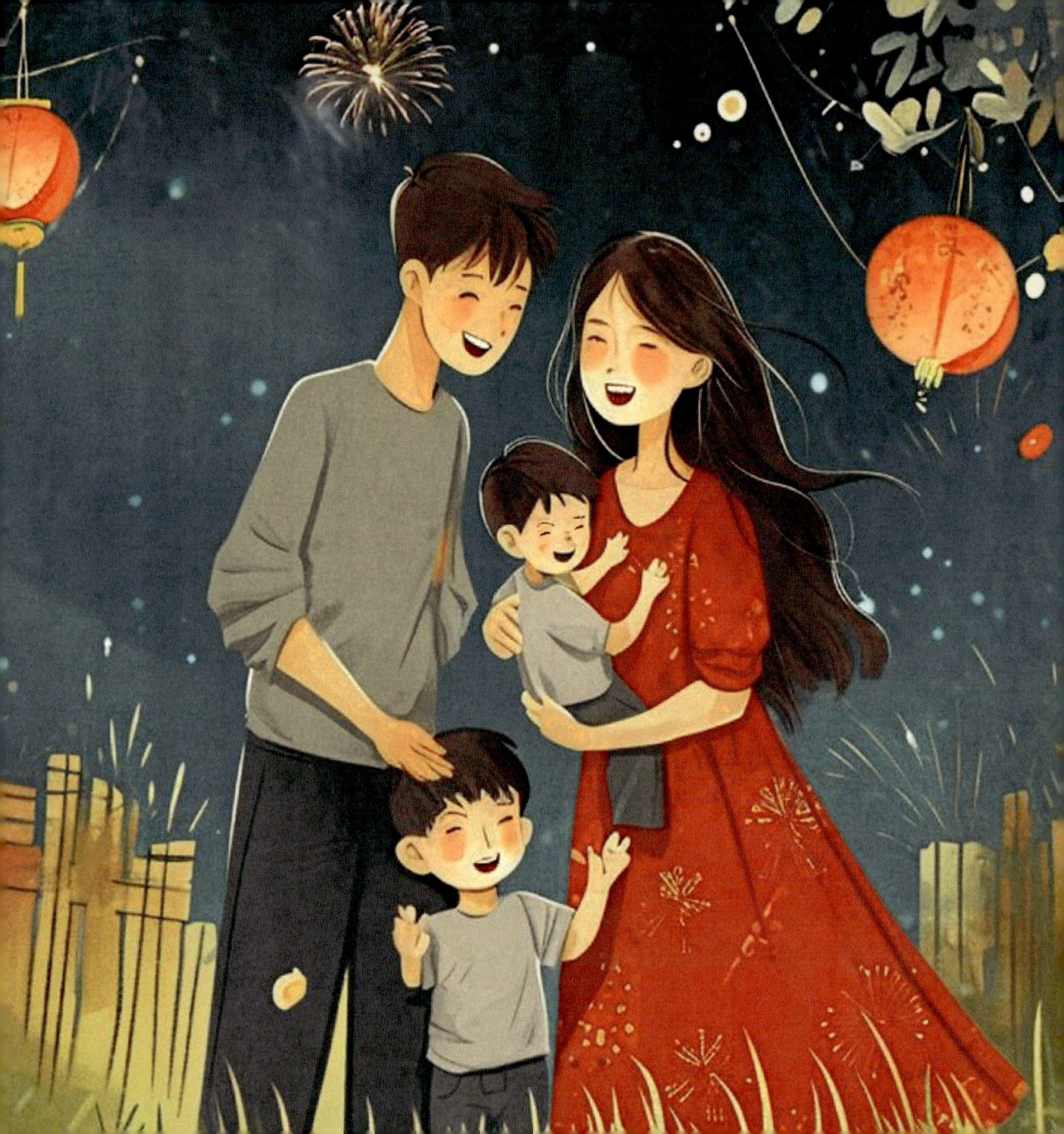

After enjoying the tale of Nian, the family goes outside to watch the fireworks. Suddenly, a dog dressed up as Nian jumps out. Nico and Keen are surprised, but then they laugh. It's their puppy, looking like Nian from the story!

在看完'年'的故事后，一家人走到外面看烟花。突然,，一只穿着'年'服装的小狗跳了出来。尼克和凯恩先是大吃一惊，然后笑了。原来是他们的小狗，装扮成故事里的年兽呢！

Hidden Challenge 小挑战

Count the total number of dragons in this book
数一数这本书里有多少条龙：_____

Fun fact: Did you know? The dragon not only looks like Nian but it's also one of the Chinese Zodiac animals.

趣味小知识：你知道吗？龙不仅外形像年兽，而且它是中国十二生肖之一。

Thank you so much for reading my first book! I had a lot of fun making this book for my children. I hope you enjoyed it. Please take a couple of minutes to leave a review on Amazon. Thank you so much for your support!

非常感谢您阅读我的第一本书！我非常开心能为我的孩子们制作这本书。希望您能喜欢。请花几分钟时间在亚马逊上留下您的评论。非常感谢您的支持！